The Flowering Woman: Becoming & Being
Copyright © 2016

Also by Q. Gibson
The Sweetness in Soil

THE FLOWERING WOMAN: BECOMING & BEING

BY Q. GIBSON

Cover design by Mario Anderson

Writing & Photography by Q. Gibson

Edited by Olga Segura and Q. Gibson

For my mother, my personal bouquet
of roses from God. For my sisters, I can't
imagine growing up in any other garden.
For my closest friends and family, thank you
for keeping me grounded. To women
everywhere, blossom, blossom, blossom—
forever.

These words do not want to share a home
inside of me anymore.

CONTENT

On Self and Being   2

On Love & Heartbreak   29

Healing, Grieving & Growing   65

On Life   88

INTRODUCTION

Lady, pull up a seat. My hands itch and open just to write these things for you. My eyes drown in salt water to release this necessary dance with sun and moon. My voice sits hallowed under my heart because sometimes these words weigh a bit too much. Have you cried lately? Have you laughed? Do you still feel? Or are you yet numb enough from being caught in the crossfire of icicles and shooting stars? Woman. Do you not know we are all the same? Fighting a universal war in chiffon and dandelion. Womanhood. It is a soft battle, it is a strong cry. It is our first nature and our native tongue. This is our silk and wool. Let us gather, let us grow, and let us dance together like flowers do. Woman, this is for you.

ON SELF & BEING

Woman.
It is sometimes all we know how to be,
and at all times the only thing we need to be.

For You

Young girl,
you walk like your feet are made
of mulberry silk and velvet.
Your hair is a river of cashmere and satin.
You rare thing,
with mahogany eyes
and a warm opulent smile.
Young Queen,
you smile like you have never shared a bed
with sorrow and thick smoke.
Your skin tells the world that tomorrow
lives happily after night breaks.
You dance and move like magnolias
are tickling at your knee caps.
Your mouth overflows with merlot
stories of celebration and life.
You wondrous thing,
golden and glowing.
Old Lady,
black opal sits swelling in your core.
Such good things,
your lips are an oyster of wisdom.
Yasmin scurries 'round your waistline.
Your ears are stuffed with Pima cotton.
You breathe like forever

has built a home inside of you.
You ancient thing,
eternal and true.
Woman,
you smell of jade and water lily.
The universe hides between your legs.
Your back is home to generations
of crocus and daisy.
Your shoulders are mansions where so much
of the world finds rest.
You wonderful thing.
You beautiful thing.
You strange, exquisite thing,
you woman.

You are beautiful, awkward, and then beautiful again. You are ever-changing and fresh each day, so don't worry too much about tomorrow. Don't worry about the days where you feel ugly; beauty is such an irresolute thing. You will break things and be broken like eggshells many times over. A limb, your heart, maybe even a finger or two. You see the beauty in breaking things is that in time they heal, and you learn a lesson engraved into every torn fiber. I pray you learn to love this life. They say it will love you back if you do. And even if it doesn't, it's the only one you get, so make it brilliant. Use your voice for good. Do away with wickedness on your tongue. Live and take a chance at everything you can't stop tossing the stinging side of your pillow for. Because in this life crazy things happen, and some wild things come true. And if you fail (and at times you will fail) at least you will grow fulfilled in knowing you have done all you have set out to do.

Signed,
Self

Drowning

Why do you leave your floating ship
to drown so much of yourself in
others?
You never come up for air alone.
You wait for them;
they wait for you to suffocate.
Is not the life jacket your mother gave you
from birth enough?
Where have you left your anchor?
Stop your drowning.
For your own sake,
stop your drowning.

You wait for things,
for men,
for people to love you,
to love yourself.
You wait for things,
for healing,
for sunshine,
to feel whole again.
You wait for things,
for life to happen,
and for it to be perfect.
You wait,
for these pages to tell you
that you are something
you have always been.
And then, you wonder
where time has gone.
Stop your waiting.

Awaiting Affirmation

When you say you love yourself
and do not mean it;
do not show it,
you are only replicating
what you've been taught.
Mirroring the same habits
you've destroyed past lovers for.
Creating a war within your soul.
Destroying yourself steadily.

Actions

Journey Yourself

Mother always told me to pack my bags and hop on a camel's back. To take nothing or no one along for the ride. "Don't make room for them," she said. The quest is not theirs at all. Store up meals and money from tear stains, and laughter so tight your stomach bulges.

Find a place to lay your head on broken ground. Use the fire you possess for warmth because you'll need it. Get familiar with blankets of sunshine and warm clay. Let your toes dance on the sands of your own heart.

Let your voice be a midnight lullaby in the dessert. Sometimes, be the river you need for crossing. Find salve behind the folding of your eyelids, when the world has left wounds on the palms of your hands. Mother always told me to pack my bags and hop on a camel's back. And though I am never alone, I am.

(My Mother's Hands)

Why must you second guess your skin?
It is home to your starlit soul;
 a sacred place for love.
You doubt its ability to protect you,
even when it is a bull's-eye
for hatred and self-pity.
It smells of cosmos and ocean salt;
it looks like everything
you didn't know you'd need.
Revel in it, glow in it and wear it like
you do at night when the moon is watching.
Flaunt it proudly, and remind your bones
each day that they dance inside something
worthy.
Be sure of it, for it is yours and only yours.

Skin

Woman,
why must we compare our skin?
Like we were ever intended to beam the
same.
White to black. Brown to tan. Light to dark.
The day gets the sun,
the night gets the moon;
and still, they are both lit.
This is the beauty of contrast.

Respect to Differences

Longing For More

You drown yourself in watered down hellos,
take pride in white hearts thumbed cherry
red.
You eat like you haven't been fed in years.
From where does your nourishment come?
You are so quick to bare your skin
before raging wolves
yet your soul to no one at all.
You live fully clothed in glass and stick,
hiding behind screens easily broken.
You smile before a million neighbors,
and live next to no one
but your fleeting shadow.
Lonely girl, lonely woman,
why do you give so much for so little?
If you are longing for more,
say it.

Pressure

Stop rushing things.
You have time to become
the woman you want to be.
In time, you will meet the person
you wish to spend forever with.
You will learn to love yourself, endlessly.
Stop pressuring yourself.
Because even though this is
the same way diamonds are made,
it is also the way most beautiful things
break.
Stop rushing things.
Because even if you don't have
as much time as you've thought,
everything that is meant for your story
will be written.

Where have your tears gone?
Have they went hiding
behind your mother's apron?
Or your father's voice?
A lover's wants?
Have they fallen faceless back into your
soul?
Retreated in a stiffened silence?
Some of the most beautiful things
come from ugly, like an ugly cry,
with little breath and weeping spit.
Who taught you that this kind
of rainfall was shameful?
Have you told your boys
that it is only for the weak?
Or whispered to your girls,
that it is only for sorrow and loss?
Have you told yourself that water
was only made for drinking?
When it has been the only thing you've ever
known to take away your dirt and blood.
Be a well, be well.

Feel

Dear woman,
feel all that you can feel.
When it hurts, let it hurt.
When you are tired, seek rest.
If you are hopeful, be.
Dear woman,
smile even when the cameras are off.
Cry massive tsunamis if you need to.
Laugh until your throat is champagne filled.
When you are mad,
scream echoes into a pitch black sky.
When you are joyful, tell the world.
When love strikes, stand in the way.
If you are scared, take the leap.
When you are frustrated,
release all of the pressure.
And know that because of this,
you are a gem.
And because of this
you are human.

Woman,
Who else could make whole persons
from the fiber of their bellies?
Feed generations of children
straight from their bosoms?
Who else could go to sleep in red sea
and wake up to daffodils?
Bend backward and still remain
upright simultaneously?
Could you break like we do?
Would you dare bleed for this long?
Rip and tear like we do
and somehow still remain whole?

The One In Question

Do not spoil yourself dying to be everything
this world
expects you to be. Sweet thing, this is how
you preserve
yourself.

Making Jam

A Soft Emancipation

After the storm settled, I dressed up in an orchid dress of lace and swept my hair back into a sort of low bun kissing the side of my neck. I figured the strands of free flowing hair I would normally leave dancing near the edge of my cheekbone should finally be put in their place because there was something very different about tonight. I pulled out a set of all black undergarments and slipped them on. You see, on the nights where I didn't wear any I'd always seemed to have forgotten myself. I covered my ears in mothers twenty-year-old diamonds, smeared my lips in a tint of raspberry and smelled like the ocean; moving like I had been washed in warm sea.

I remember sucking laboriously on a peppermint. Possibly to wash away the stench of bygones on my breath that had always tried seeping back in up through my nostrils. I slipped into grandmother's old leather trench, wrapped the belt firmly around my waist; gripping me like the very hands it had taken years for me to cut loose. My lips slipped out a tranquilizing sigh as I opened the door and fell into the calm of night. I hopped into my car and rode for what seemed like an hour to old jazz tunes and melodies of soft emancipation.

When I finally arrived at the party, the room was filled with faces of people who were dancing to the very same tunes I had rode in on. I walked in slow and stood there, right in the middle of clear souls and unshackled feet. Sure enough, my legs began to flow like they used to. Arms swaying like currents in the air; eyes shut, head tilted back, and throat humming. Smelling of the sea; of new and fresh. I felt like the water, both fluid and free. Danced like the rain, as my feet tapped the broken stone. I opened my eyes and realized that everyone else in the room had been doing the same.

Give to Give

Have you given to yourself everything you have tried giving to others? You know, all of yourself, crammed into a jam jar and packaged with everything syrupy and nectarous given to you from your ancestors.

Have you made yourself a bed of dandelion and luminescence, then promised to give one more shot at yourself when the night calls your name for a bedtime story? Before you lie down, do you pray for yourself like you'd prayed for the people you promised to speak to God about? You both need it.

Have you lent your own recipe for a Bundt cake of felicity, given yourself sugar to borrow, and then allowed yourself to finger lick the last of what goodness is left to taste because you knew your mouth had longed far enough for something sweet? Spent your last good dollar to buy back peace and reticence before anyone could fix their lips to ask? Maybe you haven't, maybe you never will and maybe you should.

I do not give myself easily and that is ok. Nor do I desire to take myself away from those who have had the pleasure of experiencing my beauty, it is their doing. I have learned to give myself without giving all of me. I have learned to take without taking away. I have learned that it is ok to save my honey for someone sweet, even if I have already given drops of it to some of the wrong people.

Giving Honey

When you are busy waiting for
others to love you,
you are waiting
to love yourself.

Your space is a privilege. It is the intangible home you have built with sweat, tears, and blood. Your space is sacred. It is not a place for people to come and go as they please. Everyone doesn't need access.
Greet them at the front door, and then, proceed with caution.

Spaces

When you finally find yourself & belong to yourself, celebrate.

If someone would have taught me how to find myself these are the things they may have said...

1. You won't find it in anyone else.
2. Going backward or in circles is definitely not the way.
3. You need **light** to do so.
4. Stop looking in the places where you lost yourself.
5. You'll have to know lonely first.
6. It'll take some time.
7. You'll have to go searching alone.

Some days will be war and others will be truce. This is
all a part of loving yourself.
Battle

ON LOVE & HEART- BREAK

The kind of love that starts as a belly pitted butterfly then becomes a whole sea.
Maturation

Loving you is a freeing occupation;
I am fearless in the way I love you.
And though loving you is everything,
it takes everything in me to be this way.

A Fearless Work

Relax into your singleness. Enjoy it. Snuggle up inside of yourself and spread love like a flame playing hooky from uncertainty and desperation. Take time with yourself, you are not ruined. You are exactly who and what you need to be in this very hour. Don't tell yourself that love has overlooked you; the most deeply rooted flowers take longer to surface and feel the sunlight. So keep growing, keep building, and continue to create stories your future lover will take a backseat to amusement for. Stories for which your lover will sacrifice; just to have an earful of all of the things you were, before you found each other.

Relax

Some only want to be wanted,
 not loved.
I want to be loved
and left alone with
myself,
until I have abandoned
the desire to be
wanted.
And then,
wanted for that.

Abandon

When *he* wakes you up super early with an unspeakable glare, roll over and be glad. When *he* sits there beaming and staring into your lovely face, although you have not had time to cover up your imperfections and sorrows from the night before, smile hard. When *he* kisses your skin softly giving you a glow that is utterly unimaginable, be grateful. When *he* goes out of his way to illuminate your entire universe, be at peace. When *he* uses his boundless energy, just to make sure you have enough to get through the height of the day, say thank you. If *he* leaves at night with you wondering where *he* has gone and how soon *he* will return, rest assured that *he* is always coming back to you. And though *he* does the same things day in and day out, it takes everything for *him* to do these things—for you.

The Sun or Someone's Son

And when I am finally in love, you'll know.
His name will sit dangling its feet
 on the ends of my tongue.
You'll notice his smile in the way
my lips curl at the very ends.
My hands will tell how
they've touched a lion's skin
and haven't been bitten.
My skin will have a glow
 that even water could not give.
Somehow, his past will disappear
 into the shadows of my teeth.
My lips will smell of a morning breeze.
There will be a fragrance of calla lilies
living in the midst of my hair.
Our eyes will meet for the first time, every
time.
My feet will stop,
 toes touching with his,
and they will say, "We are finally home".
You'll Know.

I've built a room for the one
who tends to my soul.
Cleans my mind
before getting hands dirty from skin.
Showers me daily with immeasurable love.
Lights a candle when I am dark and uneasy.
Prepares meals from conversations
we can get full on for days.
Sweeps me off of my feet
in a cliché type manner,
and then washes his hands of all things past.

The House Keeper

You look at my body like I live here,
like I've come here to stay.
If this is the only place you want to explore,
leave.

More Than a Body

My heart finds rest between the syllables of your name. It rolls off of my tongue like water. Embedded in my belly and shouting forever through my lips with every spoken vowel and consonant. Articulating eternity in every calling. I am fluent in you. Without hesitation, you are my language. "Love," I'd like to thank your mother for that.

The Name He Was Given

Find you a man who isn't afraid to flower;
to smell like softness when you need it.
One whose heart dances
to the wind in your voice.
One who isn't afraid
of the rain falling between his ears.
Find one with sunlight living in his bones.
One who is rooted, grounded deeply,
and one who isn't afraid to stand
beside you as the seasons change.

Picking Flowers

When you have a natural chemistry with someone, don't do it any harm with force. Embrace what's pure. Go with the flow. Because the thing about genuine love is, it will be what it wants when it wants, for however long it is welcome.

You Can't Rush A Good Thing

You tried to create it, didn't you?
To make something good out of thin air.
Tried to use your thighs to mold it,
your lips to speak it into existence.
You tried and I get it.
But woman,
the truth is,
you can't *make* love.
Either it's there or it isn't.

No In Between

Double the Truth

Remember the girl you fought for that man.
Neither of you wanted or needed him.
You only wanted to win.
You wanted to cut back and show
that your mother did not birth weak.
You wanted to be more secure with yourself.
You wanted her to feel how he made you
feel.
You both knew you deserved more
but instead, you fought for less.
Curdled by the fact
that you shared the same lips.
You slept drowning in the same bed,
tasted the same tears.
You tried to make sense of it, didn't you?
Tried to give reason to principles.
You tried to make so much
of a bad girl out of her,
just for him to see the good in you.
Remember the girl you fought for that man.
Neither of you wanted or needed him.

Get this,
there is no perfect man.
There are only the men we choose to love
and the men we choose not to.
There are the men we choose to tolerate
and those we don't.
There are the men we accept as they already
Are
and can stand alongside to watch
come into themselves,
just as they watch us come into ourselves.

Two Imperfect

The type of man I want….
Likes flowers.
Gives flowers.
Smells like a flower.
Feels like a flower.
Not afraid to be a flower.
Can I Grow With You?

I think we begin to truly know love when things that don't typically appeal to us start to peel back layers of selfishness, ego, and pride. We start to see that thorns are what make the roses. That scars don't take away from the beauty. We begin to see that tear stains are truly gold smudges of triumphs and that little nicks on the surface of diamonds don't make them any less valuable. We learn that nothing or no one is perfect, and knowing this frees up space for all kinds of love and boundless joy.

Accepting Imperfection

I'd be both soil and sunlight for you if you let me.
I can grow you.

Be With the One

He told me that if I didn't learn to keep my lips shut that we could never be. Tried to teach me that addressing his wrongs would leave no room for anything right. You see submission doesn't mean doormat, and love is not war contrary to popular belief. It is song and dance. It is an open window. It is a speaking mouth to an open ear. It is a battle fought endlessly together, not for eternity in opposition. Be with the one who finds a deep comfort in your voice, solace in your correction and a melody in your favorite tune.

Falling in love is something I simply do not long to do. What is the fun in that? Tripping, getting hurt, landing aimlessly. Getting scraped up, bruised, and wounded possibly. There's been enough falling into things; rushing into things and ultimately being left to clean up the blood and tears alone after the wounds have come to stay with scar tissue. I'm ready to rise.
To stand up to love,
to look up to it;
feel tall in it.
Why don't we just rise in love, together?

The Rise

What Love Feels Like

Last night I slept peacefully on a white sand cloud. My toes twinkled in between my nanas breath and snowflakes. I could hear my late grandfather say, "good morning" as the sun kissed the back of my right shoulder. As I stood up and caught my balance I looked up, and the galaxy was there. I was floating somewhere I'd never been; in a pitch white smelling of gardenia and fresh rain. I could taste a lingering whiff of sugar and ivory as I opened my mouth to say, "hello." I'd wondered how the birds got so high up that they felt the need to sing me a morning tune. My hair tied and smelling of softness and amity, I started to dance to Cosmo and King. Just as my favorite part peaked I opened my eyes, and there you were. Laying right next to me. I laughed easy and thought to myself, this must be what love feels like.

They See Us

They ask if we have dreamt of white dresses
and cotton white veils since birth.
If we have dreamt of picket fences and
moonlight
since our mother's milk.
Not how early we have seen the men leave
or how swift they have come.
They don't ask if we'd like to be anything
other than mothers and warriors.
They don't ask if the fighting is over
or how long it took the wounds
to become butter-filled.
They look at us and see a firefly in waiting.
A medallion for the ones with a sweet tooth.
These are not the ones we desire.
The ones who only see us
as sugar and caramel.
We are an acquired taste truly.
A strange and learned thing.

Reasons you settled....

1. You were too tired of waiting.
2. Everyone else had found their shooting star but you.
3. It wasn't everything you'd wanted but it was enough to make you stay.
4. You thought that love would visit again—even if your lover no longer opened the door.
5. You weren't too sure you deserved anything more.
6. You learned to like less.
7. Comfort made you feel at home in the wilderness.
8. Your mother liked it, and so did your father.
9. The years were too many all at once.
10. Something used to glow there and you wanted to play with fire again.
11. You told yourself the children needed stability.
12. Nothing was ever stable.
13. Honestly, it was all you knew.
14. You didn't want to let go.

15. It was the easiest part of what you knew about life.
16. And much easier than learning to love yourself.

When love leaves wish it well. Even though it tried to creep out the back door and did not know you were up at 3 am waiting. Send it off with kisses and warm blankets. Let it know that if it ever needs to talk your phone number will always be the same. Then close the door and don't look back. You see a love that leaves a warm home will always wish to return. And sometimes they do, only to find that you have moved into an entirely new space.

My Home Isn't Your Home Anymore

When you are exiled of
softness and love letters,
hands weary of
picking up cactus and shell,
feet scorched from walking
'round a pitied inferno,
buy yourself a ticket to familiar land
with promising fruit and fireflies.
Leave all of the memories you've built.
Leave whatever is tainted with fire,
and go. Honey, you'll never find a home
in a place that doesn't welcome you.

Gone for Good

They say I'd bent deep
and sat low for you,
folded flat like a half step.
Twisted heart strings blue,
made melodies out of silence.
Either way, you've helped shape me.
And now,
I'm unbreakable.
Definite

Ten things about the man you will truly love:

1. He won't be intentional, well at least at first.
2. He will mess up and make new.
3. He'll be both rainstorm and rainbow.
4. He will see in you what you cannot.
5. Forget an open book, he's the library.
6. He too needs space.
7. He will love you very deeply.
8. You'll never have enough words.
9. He might leave.
10. He might stay.

He knew you were enough when he had
you.
You could tell by the way he held you.
But what he also knew,
was that he himself was not yet enough.
That it was better to let you go,
then to wait for never.

That's Love

Ugly Infatuated Things

Some things start beautifully
and we watch them wither.
Some things just start
and we can't quite figure out how.
Whether they are a stunning thing or not
entirely eludes us.
We miss the beginning
and sometimes everything in between.
We stop, only to notice what has begun
to dry up and leave.
Missing the places where beautiful became
ugly;
and the spaces where our fingers
never quite fit together.
You see I think it's funny
how I keep dried roses;
because I've never had a problem
with letting things go.
But I guess the more beautiful things are,
the harder it gets.
And we were only ugly. My God were we
ugly.

Truth is,
I am just not willing
to give up loving myself
in order for you to love me.

Truth or Dare

The truth is, he never loved you.
You were only a bed of comfort
and home cooked meals.
He never loved you,
but each night he dared himself
to let you rest on an iron chest.
Is it true you knew these things?
And yet you searched for shelter
in a ransacked soul.
You dared yourself too;
smiling right side up at day
then upside down at daybreak.
You see, the truth is you are enough.
Even when you're empty and running
on the bit of self you've put away
for when the storm decides to auction
another heart.
I dare you to believe even a particle of that,
and store it with every bit of yourself you'd
left waiting.
See sometimes we lie to ourselves,
time and time again
only to begin to believe it true.
Just like we hurt each other,
time and time again

then dare to call the pain love.

Taken

Darling,
If you are ever taken by someone who does
not care for your heart wisely, return to
yourself quickly. Do not wait around for the
sun to come up underground. Don't be eager
to tie down what needs freeing. Darling, do
not wait for rage to send a heavy foot to
greet the back of your spine and then smile.
Return home, before the darkness finds you
dreaming and sleeping in a place you do not
yet belong. Return to yourself. Darling, I
beg of you, return to yourself.

Gone Missing

It is ok to miss someone. To miss the awkward laughter you shared in between days of silence and volcanic text messages. To miss the time you've spent sitting tableside with warm meals and framed pictures of half love in a home that is empty of a heartbeat. Scarfing down broccoli and a goulash of unsaid words, mixed with tears, sliding down the backs of your throats. Creating a deeper hatred in your bellies, a simmering fire in your eyes. It is ok to miss the warmth of human heat on the nights where your lingerie does not give you the fervor you thought it would. To miss the years you've spent together just to have someone stick close. It is ok to miss, to remember and to weep. But do not confuse this familiar longing for the right kind of love. Instead, wait for it.

The Things Our Mothers Teach

My grandmother taught me
to never let a man eat the last of anything.
My mother taught me that sometimes
it is ok to give a man your last.
My grandmother taught me
that the only good man is God himself.
My mother taught me
that there are still good men;
even if they aren't the ones you've had.
My grandmother taught me that if a man
lays his hands, to make soot with your sole
in the back of his stomach.
My mother taught me to fight back with my
soul and to let God do the most fighting.
I am both of these women, and they are each
other; in all of these ways we love deep.

HEALING, GRIEVING & GROWING

Heartbreak, sadness, and pain
is essential to ever knowing what it is like
to reside amongst gladness.

Five Things on Healing

1. Some people are a painful and slow healing. —blisters.
2. When the person you love is both bestfriend and stranger—let go.
3. It will always hurt at first.
4. Some wounds do heal if you stop picking at the surface.
5. You will be whole again.

There are places you loved to visit. Like the red café at the end of the street corner. Or the park behind that ransacked school. The city that birthed you. The home that raised you. You loved to drink warm cocoa in the eyes of an old lover. You sat singing sweet stories in the center of a brown iris. You slept well in between loaves of happy and wanderlust. You long to dance again inside a warm heart. You miss the laughs from your father's cave like belly. The warm sugar in your mother's hugs. You miss sharing a bed with your sister and waking up next to coco puffs and ironed linen. Somehow you still smell the cologne of crisp night air from that first date with the only man you've ever loved. Do you remember? Do you?
Don't become a stranger to these things.

—Go Again

Lessons

I break you, you break me.
You break me, I break you.
They break me, I break you.
They break you, you break me.
You break you, you break me.
I break me, I break you.
We are so broken, so tired;
there is nothing left to be,
but whole again.

Sometimes broken people teach broken people how to be whole again.

Losing someone or something you love isn't always a loss. The pain teaches you how to go on, how to look up, and how to survive moments where you may have very well believed you'd never breathe past your last breath together. And whether that last breath is bedside, or bottled in a kiss, or spat into a raging midnight air—you realize in time your lungs grow accustomed to surviving these types of losses. You learn to breathe on your own, more clearly and lightly. Darling, you learn. And that in itself is never a loss.

Breathing Easy

Backstory

From a very young age, I watched my mother live over two decades in a physically, mentally, and emotionally abusive relationship. As a young girl, this can be a very disheartening burden. You can feel hopeless like you aren't big and strong enough to protect your mother. Voiceless, like your cries for her departure are not being heard. Useless, like she cares for the man or the idea of love more than she cares for her own children.

These situations are a twisted display and teaching of love. They are an invisible and subconscious beginning of a wall built up against any and every man that ever tries to love you—only if you let it. We know not much about our mothers, just the things they choose to show us. Young girls may very well never understand why their mothers are tolerating or enduring these battles for some pitied idea of love. But what I do know is we learn, and we live to talk to our mothers if permitted.

We live to share, to heal, and to write about it. I urge you to look at the situations you have endured, encountered, and overcome to find gold in them. Though they may not be understood at the moment, a month after, a decade after, or even at all. These are the incidents that write your story when you didn't see them coming. These are the things that teach you to heal, to forgive, to be strong, and to grow.

Memoirs of the Man I Never Wanted to Love

On this night we sat slick-faced, huddled in a love sick hallway. Mother was dressed in all-black lingerie as if some sort of thick fog was brewing. The very hands that caressed her face were now rope dangling her from an open window. I can't remember too well what season it was, but the air from that particular window felt like a winter storm had been whispering right outside of it. The moon may have tucked its face behind some trees or light poles because not a strip of light could be found.

Everything seemed to be a blur as my four sisters and I sat numbly on stiffened ground. Though I was watching like some sort of tragic and frightful movie, I could hear nothing but a dripping silence. In an instant, I heard mother scream. And then, the sound of nothing. I take it her mind went black from the smell of tobacco and hatred sitting drunk and slumped over on her lovers' breath. His eyes didn't even have the decency to draw water for the sake of losing her.

I looked on asking myself, small and with the cloud of a thick air, what births this kind of sick and twisted love? What foul and wretched French kiss can spark this kind of hatred? As he pulled her back into what seemed to be the coldest room in our bewildered four-story jungle, I swear I'd saw her soul jump right out from behind her, plummet to the ground, and jet down the street for dear life.

You see pieces of her left him that day. And though she decided to stay, maybe mother was dressed in fact for some type of memorial. The desperate parts of me died forever that day. And I didn't stick around for the going. That day, I vowed never to settle, or to love a man anything like the one mother had decided to love. Ever.

Mama Girl

How do you go to bed under his skin
and wake up at the soles of his feet?
You lie awake in puddle stained pillows
and dare to call this thing love.
You stare into a sleeping face
hoping not to wake the devil in him.
Sleep next to knife and gun
on soiled sheets of lies and clotted love
stories.
You breathe like each breath is your last
when you're near him.
You tiptoe around
in the only house you've built.
The words "I love you" have become a ritual
of self-protection and preservation.
Mama girl, mama girl.
What are you afraid of?

What Your Mother Did

Don't fault your mother.
She has been ten,
and twenty,
and thirty,
and forty.
She has kissed the boys;
questioned her own mother.
Fell head first,
then cried herself to sleep.
She has lost it all,
then found it again.
Shared her heart with you,
even when her lips did not move.
She has written love letters in scribble
to you and your siblings;
only to be understood when you
have learned to read life well enough.
Your mother has died several times over,
for you to live many times more.

Perfect Timing

I never thought the day would come when mother would leave. When she'd finally realize her soul had shipped enough cargo and carried enough dead weight. We'd always talked about God and how his timing was perfect. But in actuality, I had lost hope of a peaceful and silent escape after twenty years of dark noise and battle.

Surprisingly the going was peaceful; without a care at all for returning. And maybe the timing was perfect because there was no talk of leaving and it seemed to be some sort of divine doing. She left untouched, which was shocking because it wasn't out of the ordinary to find that her lover had found a desperate peace in doing harm. She left without a tear. I figured she'd cried them all out by the time God had decided her fleeing was a granted one. She left without looking back, although it was something she had done time and time again.

You see leaving is not about being ready, no one is ever quite settled in doing so. And I don't think it is at all about us making the call. Because though we'd tried to do that for her time and time again, no matter the pleas it'd never come to pass. I don't think it has anything to do with the will of those who are affected because the hurt lingers; they are scarred and the cycle seems to become a strangely comfortable thing. What I do believe is that it has everything to do with timing, divinity, and when the spirit has truly had enough.

We know not all of the things we were cooking up in prayer, look how tranquil the departure was. I questioned twenty years and why it took so long. Until I began to reflect on the pain and the things that went down in cold sweat at midnight. I questioned time and its concern for a fragile and sacred life, or if mother would have any of it left after him.

I never knew why she endured any of it, or why any of it had anything at all to do with me. That was until I began to write about it. I began to write about the pain, the healing, the years, and finally the escape. And now that I am able to finally reflect all I can say is, "Wow, what perfect timing."

Dear Daddy,
I forgive you.

Dear Daddy,
I love you.

Five powerful words can be poetry to the
soul, and one can be all the healing you
need.

Forgiveness

Your body is made up of over 70% water.
You are both rain and soil,
yet you are still afraid to cry.
How else do you expect to grow?
Water Yourself

Leave the Wounds

When the wounds are first split open all we see is the turmoil. We feel every tissue and every fiber of ourselves fighting to pull it together, to become one with us again. We don't notice the invisible and minute healing going on in the midst of it all. We can't see the remedy in every ache.

As time goes on, we no longer touch and pick at it as much. We leave it to be what it is and pray the scarring is minimal, or nothing at all. We give it time, we tend to the wound with care. We don't peel back old layers or wish to open up what has already found some sort of closure. We leave it be, we stop forcing it to soothe, and we find soon enough that it has become one with us. A part of us that happened and hurt, yet it is finally whole and healed.

Learning to Swim

With good intentions, or maybe none at all we questioned the lows. Like we ought to be exempt of hitting the bottom of things and staying there a while. Like we didn't deserve to experience the ocean pouring heavily on our heads and us floating mindlessly in the lap of it for hours, days, or years even. We'd thought we were a bit too ethereal to be granted the fullness of a relentless and seemingly never-ending ocean. Found ourselves laying there, praying to come up for air and promising we'd never want to taste the ocean again if we could only get out.

But the water was deep, and we hadn't learned yet to swim in anything over five feet in a public playground. As we submerged, oh how we learned to swim on our own. Legs kicking fast, hands and arms moving freely inward and out. Holding our breath, because we knew we were on our way back up to the surface again.

Realizing we'd gotten our feet wet for far longer than we could imagine; that we'd laid there far longer than we would've liked to. But maybe the water was good for a while. It taught us to swim truly and to appreciate when the sun kisses our crown; when our breath finally lets out the wind at the surface. It taught us that maybe we aren't too much, or ever too exempt. It taught us that in time everyone, and I mean everyone, learns to swim in deep waters.

For the women who have ever dealt with postpartum depression or depression of any kind – time.

You were made to be whole again; to be
repaired after brokenness.
Look at how the liver cleanses you of
toxicity. How the skin mends itself back
together.
Be content in the heart's ability to repair
itself.
Cleanse your space,
take time for yourself,
and appreciate the process.
This vessel was created
for your soul's protection.
Take care of it and heal.

Care to Heal

ON LIFE

Dear Woman,
do not fear the labor.
Let life do its work on you.

Life as Such

There comes a time when becoming a flower gives way to a cloud of euphoria. We come into ourselves suddenly without warning. Hips begging the rest of our bodies to give way. We bud from the thighs up and blossom in all of the places our mothers once called names like pocketbook or anything similar to a feline.

We learn to be called by our birth names and tend not to tolerate any note from the tongue that ends in slander or distaste. We learn to like the lovers and to possibly dig deeper into them than we have done ourselves by the time they've let us go. We watch the sunrise from our bellies and sometimes the sun sets in the same place. We learn to smell like sunlight and to tan underneath God until we are sun kissed with a familiar grace and strength.

We get rained on when love leaves us. We find the light in ourselves. We play around in places where war has left mud and tar on the backs of our skin. And all the while we laugh, we dance, and we learn to like this heart-wrenching bliss. And oh is it

mad, and beautiful, and brilliant. This life as
a woman.

To the Woman Bearing an "Illegitimate" Child

What did you hear them say? What did they say that had you questioning yourself? Did they tell you how you could no longer journey yourself, without all the extra baggage? Or how the morning sickness wouldn't keep you from being lovesick?

Did they tell you how the men would now smell what they'd also covered up with perfume and poinsettias? Did they talk with selfishness guarded in the gates of their teeth? Or maybe they rejoiced about how pristine it made them feel.

Did they whisper that your life would now become a sea of hardship? Maybe they talked about all the pointless soirees you'd miss for a while? Or the fact that your left hand was not yet set in ruby? You see, they couldn't have told you about the night their mothers told them not to tell their fathers that they had been safe-housing a lily in the pit of their bellies.

And when the morning came they made sure to spit out before anyone could smell the blossom. Maybe they told you how your world would end. But if only they knew that this was the reason it began again.

(Mama)

To Look Like Mother

Mother, I want to look just like you.
How your skin is slow to follow your years.
Your eyes have seen so much
and yet they are light filled.
Eyelashes still double over in laughter with
every blink.
Every tress of hair entangled with strength.
Love letters engraved in the lines of your
belly
from wholly baked bread.
Feet that have walked ages of sands
yet still the consistency of fine silk.
Nails saying, "Grow."
I hear your voice in the way I talk.
I think about how your bone and blood
surrendered just enough
so that I'd come to know you inside out.
Mother, I am blessed;
because I already look just like you.

Good Garden

Surround yourselves with the flowers who yearn to see you flourish. The ones who seek sunlight just as you do and never feel slighted when you inherit its rays. The flowers who slumber in the rain with you, to help soak up anything that is overflow for balance and nourishment. Seek flowers who are long standing; those who fear not the seasons. The flowers who do not grow green from resentment and covetousness but thrive from growth and longevity.

If you have ever resided in a garden amongst flowers as beautiful as these, dream wildly and stay planted. And if you have never set foot in one as rare and special as this, travel as wide as you can with roots intact; until you find the flowers worth sharing both soil and sunrise with.

The Thing about Women

The thing I love most about being a woman is that we are like flowers in so many ways. Fragile and beautiful; rooted and lively. We are the start of life and even when we are seemingly dead, we emerge and become even more alive. There is a continual life through us. We are never ending; ever beautiful. We dry up and still possess the beauty we began with. We know growth because it is who we are. We know the power of rain and sun, sadness and happiness, and that both parts are necessary for our existence. We do not fear the rain, we welcome the sun. We do not fear the bloom, we await it in warm soil. We are flowers, we are flowers; we are all flowers.

Sometimes you don't understand the rain,
until the sunshine comes along
and reminds you of why it is necessary.
Necessary Reminders

Some people will be like a tornado. They will move swiftly with intentions of destroying everything in their paths. Fueled by their own storms and carelessly vicious with no explanation at all. They will near you, and spiral out of control. Hoping to take all you have built. So when they draw close enough to smell debris and lost life, be the sun or cloud that breaks them and puts their raging winds to rest.

Chasers

Flowers from Concrete

There are those peculiar flowers, have you
seen them? The ones that come from
concrete, a hard and stiffened place. You
tend to walk by them without care, miss
their beauty because they aren't sitting
poised in a garden next to peonies or tulips.
These are the flowers you worry about,
wishing they were given soil to begin with
like the others. You weep for them, try to
prune them, and mistake them for weeds.
They begin to bloom a bit, and you are in
awe of how they continue to sleep and push
through stone beds. You wonder if they will
ever survive the rain and ultimately they do.
They grow, they blossom, and then they
bloom in full. We are the flowers that have
survived the concrete, don't be surprised. It
is only our nature.

On Time

One day you are without breast, lying next to mother's milk singing songs her mother whispered between warm pillows and working hours. Next you are fighting battles of the skin and worrying if your hips are set in enough already. Then, you are torn in between looking good for the boys and if the boys even look good. Quickly enough you are tackling a dream and a lover. You are birthing daffodils, and singing the same songs mother sang to you in between warm pillows and working hours. You are losing friends and gaining them. Running breathless behind children, lovers, and your old self; asking if it's all ok. And it is. Then, you check the years, aching to see if you have given to them wisely without mishap. And you haven't. But it is still ok. And it is magical and worth it, and all too soon, but right in the nick of time.

Tell Your Girls

Mothers,
Tell your girls that lonely is not a curse,
that some darkness is necessary
for light to find its way.
Tell them that honeysuckle and sugar
lives between their thighs.
Then warn them, that the bees will come
searching for their sweetness.
Most days are wild roses
and others are a soft baby's breath.
Tell them, that the rain may come
for forty days and forty nights
but the sunlight always finds its way home.
Tell them that the ride home may be a long
one,
and the road can go wherever it may.
Then tell them,
to live freely, blazing,
joyful, and vivacious.
To live madly and truly
in love with their lives.

Years

In what time I've had to wander and scurry about this earth, I have found that life is not about being easy. I have found that it is not always about how high up we can get. It is about depth, and how deep we can bend ourselves into the time we have. How wholly we can fit into the hands of this world and give from the core what can be sowed on shared soil, then graciously reaped for ages. It is about the years. About losing them happily, and with peace as we become particles of dust in a lily field. All while realizing that the time, the days, and years mean nothing if we have not learned to fill them with moments in which we lose track of it all.

As I was writing I sat there thinking, "Maybe I need to take some of the hurt out of this." I thought, "Maybe I should remove some of this aching"; "Maybe the words should be all light and airy; all poised and pretty." But there was nothing poised and pretty about me that hadn't been through some hurt and aching. Nothing beautiful that hadn't been through some pain. So I left them here, for you.

Maybe you will remember to leave your words as they are; accept your story for what it is and find the beauty in it. Stop wishing to erase or cover up what has already been written and learn to smile back at the bits of life you have learned to live beyond.

I like how you came here expecting pretty,
but instead, you got pain and some sunshine.
And then, you still chose stay.
Thank you

Q. Gibson is a writer and artist born in Cleveland, Ohio. She is a graduate of the University of Toledo and currently works and resides in Reynoldsburg, Ohio with her son. *The Flowering Woman: Becoming and Being* is her debut collection of writing.

Made in the USA
Coppell, TX
20 June 2020

28587507R00066